FROM BARRIO TO BOARDROOM

A Latino Banking Executive's Fight for Racial Equality

BY ALEX VASQUEZ

CO-AUTHOR: BERT BOTTA

FROM BARRIO TO BOARDROOM

A Latino Banking Executive's Fight for Racial Equality

BY ALEX VASQUEZ

Copyright © 2022 by Alex Vasquez
All rights reserved

Author: Alex Vasquez
Co-Author: Bert Botta

No part of this book may be reproduced in any form or by any electronic or mechanical means, including information storage and retrieval systems, without written permission from the author, except for the use of brief quotations in a book review.

ISBN: 979-8825513225

FROM BARRIO TO BOARDROOM

*A Latino Banking Executive's
Fight for Racial Equality*

BY ALEX VASQUEZ
CO-AUTHOR: BERT BOTTA

DEDICATION

To my parents who taught me true life values, respect, trust and integrity.

To my wife who believed in me and my journey.

To my family internal and external who often wondered what my journey was all about.

To the workers/teammates that allowed me to support them and did all the work.

To my boyhood friends who stood close to their heritage and allowed me to be their friend.

To my Jewish-American coach and my first two bosses both African American's who had served this country and shared with me their journey's.

To all the people of color that rode that bus every workday to build a better way of life for them and their families.

To the largest Latino nonprofit advocacy group that allowed me to join them and share my experience and knowledge.

And to all the people that impacted my journey both in a positive and not so positive way. Both built my courage and dedication.

Never give up.

Alex Vasquez

TABLE OF CONTENTS

09 | Introduction: From Barrio to Boardroom: A Latino Banking Executive's Fight for Equality!

15 | Chapter 1: Born and Bred Mexican in America

23 | Chapter 2: Eyes Wide Open

25 | Chapter 3: The American Dream Takes Shape:

29 | Chapter 4: The Big Time, Bank of America

31 | Chapter 5: Moving On: Home Savings of America

35 | Chapter 6: "Magic" for Minorities!

41 | Chapter 7: The Cost of Winning

45 | Chapter 8: Retirement: Now What?

49 | Chapter 9: Clearing the Hurdles

51 | Chapter 10: The Dreamers

55 | Chapter 11: Rampant Racism

57 | Chapter 12: What's Next?

61 | Afterword

INTRODUCTION:

FROM BARRIO TO BOARDROOM: A LATINO BANKING EXECUTIVE'S FIGHT FOR EQUALITY!

Racism! The word is kicked around a lot these days. Who's a racist and who's not? Do you know if you're a racist!?

Most of us don't consider ourselves 'racist'. But racism is often very subtle, like justifying a "slight prejudice" against people of color by saying "that's just the way it is."

This kind of racism remains essentially invisible but it's often felt without knowing where and how to look for it, how to deal with it, how to end it.

Since that could be the case, I want this book to educate and inspire you so you don't have to repeat the mistakes I made.

My hope is that my book will act as a kind of "racial road map" for you.

OUR STORY?

My name is Alex Vasquez, and this is my story but... it very well could be yours! But it's more than just my story. It might be more about you, my reader if you're a person of color. This is a book of possibilities, hidden possibilities if you don't know where to look.

I want this book to not just provide you with knowledge but I want it to educate and inspire you.

Educate those of you who may have no idea of the kind of "hidden" prejudice and racism that goes on in all levels of the business world.

Inspire those of you who might think there's no way out from under the subtle but very effective oppression that keeps people of color "treading water" and unable to get ahead.

MY STORY?

I'm an American-born Mexican. I retired from Corporate America 4 years ago, and this is the story I've needed to tell for a long time!

My journey of 50 years took me many places. I made mistakes, I won some fights, I lost some. But I learned a lot.

I want to pass on what I learned so those of you who can benefit from my wins, my losses and my mistakes so you will have a kind of "racism road map" to navigate around the racial, cultural and financial potholes.

This is important since, without my hard-fought

experience to fall back on you may not even know you're headed into the ditch!

I had great street smarts; it was part of growing up in East Los Angeles. I got business smarts on the job. Over time they grew together.

My background and experience are in Consumer Finance, Banking and Mortgage.

In business and in life I always fought for equality. And I always seemed to end up fighting for the people that no one cared about. They weren't hard to find.

That fight was never easy, but I knew that I could never give up. When I retired, I figured I could relax, take a break, the fighting was over.

I was wrong.

I was wrong because between the years of 2016 and 2020 the messaging of hate, displeasure and a long history of negativity from right-wing individuals and extremist groups came alive. This gave a platform to extremist groups throughout the country.

I don't have a platform. I'm not a celebrity, I'm not a professional athlete, I'm not a member of a left- or right-wing group and I don't have a college degree.

Who I am is a person of integrity and trust who worked hard through a career of highs and lows.

I'm an American of Mexican descent.

I was faced with discrimination and racism in all forms from people who I never suspected were that way.

I was wrong.

I want my story to be a voice of awareness. Latinos, Hispanics and all people of color cannot be taken for granted. We are a strong part of this country, and we are an integral part of its history.

You may think you're in a good place but maybe you're not.

Just be awake and move forward with your journey. You'll get there…just be aware of the forces at work against you.

FOUNDATIONS

My story is my foundation. I knew all along that I could still help. I knew that I could still make a difference.

So why is this important to you?

People of color are growing in huge numbers in America. Families are growing and ties to communities are stronger than ever.

But as I moved around the country, I saw a gap that needed to be addressed.

It was an equality gap. Equality in wealth, housing, education, health care and community participation.

Retiring gave me some breathing room, a chance to look around and focus on where I could help.

WEALTH AND THE AMERICAN DREAM

Wealth for most Americans comes from home ownership. That represents most American's Dream.

I lived in poor neighborhoods, middle class neighborhoods and later, in upscale neighborhoods. I saw a lot, learned a lot because I saw through the mirage of what others saw as "reality."

In the middle-class neighborhood I lived in, the police were called because a resident reported us as "not belonging there!" I was repairing a brick wall on my property, and they assumed I was a worker and could no way own the house!

In the upscale community, I was doing some remodeling and I had a city inspector come up to me and ask me to go get the owner so that he could go over the permit plans. Again, the assumption was that as a person of color I could not own a home in those communities.

The resident who reported me and city planner were white.

So be awake, know what's going on and have good "situational awareness" so you can be prepared. Through it all, be strong.

Since I retired, I've been reaching out to see where I could help those who were just starting their journey. Those who were seeking their own version of the American Dream.

I want to teach them, people just like you who are reading this. I want to share and encourage you. I want you to know that this is your country and that you can reach that Dream of…

- Equality
- Homeownership
- Wealth

In my search I found an organization that, through them, I could help.

But first, some history…

CHAPTER 1:

BORN AND BRED MEXICAN

IN AMERICA, 1951-1969

I was born and raised in East Los Angeles in the "Boyle Heights" neighborhood. My dad was born in El Paso Texas, Mom was born in San Bernardino California. My Dad served his country in World War II while my mom was a stay-at-home Mom.

After the war my father had several jobs, sometimes 2 or 3 at a time so he could provide for our family. He sent all us kids to Catholic schools, grades 1-12.

He finally ended up with a good career, working 30 years for the Sears and Roebuck chain where he retired as a supervisor. There's no doubt he's where my dedication, integrity and commitment come from.

I have two brothers and two sisters. I was the second youngest in the family. My oldest brother was a jock, and my dad was very proud of him. My other brother was also a good athlete, and he did well with his studies. They both were mentors to me and strong leaders.

My older sister has a great heart and is a very good person. She always looked out for and cared for me. My younger sister are years apart in age.

I lived on Winter Street in Boyle Heights. I had 3 good friends, Alfred, Tony and Sal. I was the oldest by a year or two. We all went to the same elementary and high school. As we grew up, I found myself becoming the leader of the block.

I think there were a couple of reasons for that. One was because I was older, and I had older brothers. My friends didn't have any brothers, only sisters so I figure my buddies looked up to me as their older brother.

Our days consisted of playing street ball and just hanging out. I always took the lead in sports. If it was baseball, I pitched, if it was football, I was the quarterback and when we played basketball I did it all.

The other kids' parents came to America from Mexico. They all had strong cultural ties. They all spoke Spanish and very little English, but all eventually became bilingual. Looking back today, that was a beautiful thing.

My parents didn't want us to speak Spanish because they wanted us to blend in, to be fluent in English. They felt that was the ticket to the American Dream, as did all the other families.

GRADE SCHOOL: SHAPING A LEADER

Grades 1-4 at Our Lady of Assumption Catholic School was the same for everybody. It was a school that believed in God and the United States and these were my foundation years, years that taught me the respect and structure that I needed to be an American.

Grades 5-8 is where I started to see things a little different.

We prayed and recited the "Pledge of Allegiance" every morning. I was taught by Catholic nuns, women that dedicated their lives to God and the Church.

We had two Catholic priests that worked closely with the school. The Pastor worked with the families and his associate worked with the school. As far as I knew there was no priest abuse but that was obviously not the case in other places.

I was heavily involved in sports, and they played a major role in my life during this time. I won honors in both flag football and basketball. During these years we were coached by a Jewish-American named Archie Lifland.

I smile when I think back on the fact that we went to a Catholic school that was predominately Hispanic and we were coached by a Jewish American!

Archie taught me a lot even though he only coached me through the 7th grade. One of the things that stuck with me were the "3 D's", Desire, Determination and Defense. He taught me that there were lessons to be learned from winning and losing. I never realized all along that he was teaching us about life and the importance of never giving up.

Archie, a Jewish-American helping Hispanic kids was a lot like the block I lived on. The street was diverse; it was a real American melting pot; we had Italian, German, Asian and Jewish neighbors.

Around this time, I realized that life was not always

perfect, far from it! I remember seeing a sign in school prohibiting us to speak Spanish on campus. Even though most of the students where bilingual there were no cultural studies, celebrations or acknowledgments of our Spanish culture or heritage.

As far as we knew, brown and black people had no history. Even Jesus Christ was white with blue eyes. Looking back, we knew that was wrong.

During those years, history changed dramatically for the United States; one of the most shocking, sad things that happened during that time was the assassination of President John F Kennedy.

JFK was a Godsend for Latinos. He recognized us, he spoke to us, he made us feel special; he made us feel like we were a real part of the United States.

So real that many Latino homes honored JFK by displaying his portrait alongside a portrait of Our Lady of Guadalupe. A beautiful show of love and respect.

Our admiration for JFK was so real that I recall a rally where my dad, brother and I ran after his motorcade so we could just get a glimpse of the man that would include us in the American story.

HIGH SCHOOL: A NEW WORLD

When I started high school, I had to ride public transportation; that meant leaving the comfort zone of my neighborhood; that was the beginning of my "eyes wide open" phase.

In the summer before I started my freshman year,

I found my first job. I joined the National Youth Corp. It was a national program that provided jobs for inner city kids. I was assigned to the Catholic Church of the Stars, Blessed Sacrament.

My job was a "helper" to the janitor of the church, an African American man who had served his country and now was on his path to the American Dream. To get to work I rode public transportation from East Los Angeles to Hollywood and Beverly Hills.

This job opened my eyes even further; by taking the bus every day and working there, I saw different people living very different lives than mine; this was a very different world than the one I was used to.

Riding that bus, I saw people of color going to work, all pursuing the American Dream, even though if I had stopped to ask them if that's what they were doing, they would probably have no idea what I was talking about!

For them it was all about working hard to provide for their families and offering them a chance for a better way of life.

Riding through those neighborhoods I began to see special privilege up close and personal; fancy, expensive cars, huge well-kept houses and businesses to name just a few examples. As I looked closer at those homes, cars and businesses, I saw they were owned by white people.

I didn't understand how or why this happened. I started asking questions.

My African American boss told me that difference is what the struggle is all about. He often shared with me that I should always be aware of what I was facing and be prepared. It was later in my journey that I fully understood what he was telling me.

THE NEW KID IN SCHOOL

Starting the school year was exciting. Cathedral High School was a predominately Latino high school not far from downtown Los Angeles and just down the hill from Dodger Stadium. I got good grades there and played some sports.

This was the same school that my brothers attended and had left a strong legacy; my legacy would be different.

As a freshman I met kids from different parts of the city. This one kid who came from a very tough black neighborhood was a great athlete. He was the future of our football team. I saw that but I also saw that he struggled in class.

Our instructor asked him who would he trust to help him with his studies; he requested my help. He didn't get much help or support from his home, so I was it.

We worked hard together on his studies. He got it and he moved on. He was grateful and I was thankful.

As it turned out, when I helped him, it was helping me in some way. That beginning year was a good one for me in sports. I started on the defensive line in football.

During the season I convinced my coaches that I could make more tackles if I could stand up and rush the other team. It worked; I made more plays than my teammates. In basketball I was a starting guard, I did well, and we did well. That was a big deal for me and for the Freshman team.

But things began to change the next three years. I played one more year of sports, my grades continued to be ok, but I was beginning to see favoritism and cliques, inner circles in many places. That was when I started seeing people with less talent get opportunities that people of color and more talent weren't offered.

That was also when I began to see people of color being treated unfairly; it was at that point that I decided to confront that kind of treatment.

It was also then that I decided to work every day after school.

I got a job with the government, working as a postal assistant in another national school program. I did that up through graduation and beyond. That job gave me some money that I was able to help my family with; it also helped me get a broader picture of the world.

That job also taught me a lot about people in leadership positions. I learned some valuable lessons from some very senior government employees, people of color.

Like my boss at the Church of the Stars, my Post Office boss was another African American man who served his country; he shared with me his journey thru racism and prejudice. He offered direction and support and made sure that I understood that the journey would take strength and courage.

CHAPTER 2:

EYES WIDE OPEN

The idea of college was better than the reality; it didn't work for me.

I continued working and I took a job for a financial company in downtown Los Angeles. The job was nothing special, but it opened my eyes to the differences between management and the employees; management was white, workers were people of color.

But the big deal at the time, especially in Los Angeles, was the financial companies' softball league. The company I was working for played in this league, but the team had no real talent. So, me and several of my fellow workers, all people of color, were encouraged to join the team.

As soon as we started playing, we started winning! We won first place in the league that season. My brown and black teammates talked about what had just happened. What we accomplished. And how we were now being recognized.

We got the picture; when we were needed, we were asked to join; when we weren't needed, we were ignored.

History had already shown us this. In the 1800's the then Senator from South Carolina made it clear about Mexicans in the work force, "As for Mexicans we never dreamt of incorporating them into the Union". "Ours, Sir is the government of a white race".

During the 70's social struggles were hitting their stride.

Like the BLM movement, some 50 years earlier the same type of protests were taking place in Los Angeles.

In 1970 I marched in the East Los Angeles Chicano Moratorium. Protesting the Vietnam war and other injustices being done to people of color. I was on the same street that saw LA Times Journalist Rueben Salazar shot and killed by the LA County Sheriffs. There was never an investigation or charges brought against the sheriffs.

50 years later things are about the same.

I continued to learn what the differences were and what it would take to move forward.

I knew that through dedication and hard work I could move on to a better place; that shaped my journey.

CHAPTER 3:

THE AMERICAN DREAM TAKES SHAPE: ALL STATE INSURANCE COMPANY, 1976-1988

Because of my solid background and experience in finance I was hired at All State Finance, a division of All State Insurance.

I was 25 at the time, with no college degree and here I was working for a major corporation. That was more than luck because by now I knew that my hard work was paying off.

MY VERSION OF THE AMERICAN DREAM

The lessons that I was learning were bringing me closer to my version of the American Dream.

I was being trained in Consumer Lending; that would open some doors for me, but it also opened my eyes to the "haves and haves not" of the business world. It was clear that financial inequality was the reality that people of color were facing whether they knew it or not.

I was also learning about equal opportunity and affirmative action but at the same time I learned that Latinos weren't included in either!

I knew why. Because at that time Corporate America had this vision that if they could demonstrate positive activity of reaching out to the African-American community then community organizations like the Urban League and NAACP would look past their abuses of people of color. At least that's what they were hoping for.

But I knew historical Latino organizations like The American GI Forum and LULAC (League of United Latin American Citizens) were beginning to create the same pressure, so it was just a matter of time. I knew I had to do my part.

My work results were outstanding. I knew I had a future here. But I was also witnessing discrimination and favoritism and I knew that Latinos and people of color were being ignored, pushed aside for promotions as less qualified persons got the promotions and opportunities.

I felt that I needed to make a statement because I was working for this corporation and seeing first-hand the discrimination and prejudice that was taking place.

In an awareness paper that I delivered to All State Senior leaders, I offered solutions that I felt would help solve the discrimination that I was seeing and experiencing. That document put me in a position to help see the kind of prejudice that was taking place in the corporate world and in the country.

Management saw something in me that prompted them to send me to the home office. It was here that I was able to help place Latinos into the affirmative action program. My excitement led to the beginning of a longer struggle.

In the debates I had with the white leaders I made it clear that the fact that we were all working toward the American Dream could be very good for business.

I built training and knowledge programs for white leaders that had an effect… sometimes!

I formed partnerships with non-profits and built training programs for Latino college students to better prepare them for life in the business world. That had a ripple effect in the community, and I was finding that my reputation would often precede me!

It was at this point that I realized I had done all I could do and, after 12 plus years with Allstate, I left for another challenge, this one just as great!

CHAPTER 4:

THE BIG TIME: BANK OF AMERICA, 1989-1995

This was big for me: I was hired at Bank of America to help change the culture! Because of a lack of empowerment by the bank, their traditional bankers lacked the skills and knowledge how to drive the kind of revenue that they needed.

With my consumer lending background and my corporate partnerships, and in partnership with Enterprise Rent a Car, I built and delivered the first Tent Car sales.

I partnered our Lending Officers with Enterprise Leaders and sold cars through consumer loans. As a result of that partnership our sales numbers were higher than anything the bank had ever seen!

From there I took over the management of a bank branch in a Latino community. Through building awareness and training I took them from a poor sales record to one of the highest revenue driven banks in Southern California.

These kinds of results had never been seen before. Because of this, the surrounding cities and communities brought business and savings to this branch.

What was crucial in the growth of this bank was the employees who were mostly Latinos realizing, for the first time ever, that they were valuable to the success of the bank, not only to the branch but to their families and to the families in their community. To me the beginning of success was Latino's building pride and strength.

CHAPTER 5:

STEADY PROGRESS: HOME SAVINGS, 1996-2005

As my journey evolved, my passion for business was contagious; the mortgage industry allowed me another path toward the American Dream.

I joined Home Savings of America to further develop my lending skills with the idea of helping Latinos gain home ownership and to also give people of color a chance to reach their American Dream. As my knowledge grew, I was able to build strong partnerships with our sales and service partners while leading teams of mortgage underwriters, processors and closers.

In my work with both upscale and minority markets - with upscale markets being mostly white and minority markets being mostly people of color - I saw the differences in approval ratings between those markets soar.

That often involved me having to fight for what I saw was right. I won some, I lost some.

I saw and experienced the difference between the

privileged inner circle and the redlining of people of color. This was just the beginning of a long but important fight.

THINGS WERE GOING SOUTH!

The fight required helping families of color realize their dream of home ownership. UGI, also known as United Guaranty Insurance Company, provided Mortgage Insurance for homeowners who put less than a 20% down payment for a home. That insurance was designed to protect the lender, not the borrower.

Having gained valuable knowledge through one of the largest mortgage lenders in the country, Home Savings of America, it was now time to take that strength to one of the largest Mortgage Insurance companies in the country.

I was a Contract Leader with a team of Latino underwriters and processors at UGI; I was responsible for determining the risk of the applicant for a home loan.

Many applicants of color were now getting a real chance to be homeowners. I felt that we were making a difference; so did the UGI Corporation.

As this team grew in production, I was offered a meeting with the CEO in Charlotte North Carolina. The West coast operation saw an opportunity to capture the growing Latino market and they knew that I could make that happen. I put together an action plan with a timeline to move UGI towards capturing that market.

In the process of being sent to North Carolina from UGI to meet with their CEO, my job was to help him increase minority lending by putting together a plan to make that happen.

As it turned out, the plan was accepted by everyone except the CEO!

I flew to Charlotte and met with several Senior Executives. My presentation was well received, and all the leaders wanted to move forward. My face-to-face meeting with the CEO was next. It was a very different story and not pretty!

The CEO was white, and our meeting took place around his late lunch. He asked me if I wanted to eat. I told him no, I wasn't hungry, but he should go ahead and enjoy. I continued with the same presentation I had been giving all day.

He listened as I spoke, but I could see that he wasn't following me. What I also saw was that throughout that entire time he was being served by Latinos. His food, his drink, his fork, his cup, his glass - everything was being brought to him by Latinos.

I could see that, in his head he's thinking "How could this brown guy sitting across from me be one of my leaders?" When all he saw were brown people in a subservient role?

That's exactly what the meeting turned out to be, a white leader who couldn't and didn't want to visualize an opportunity to allow people of color to grow in the industry as leaders much less as homeowners.

He had no plans to carry out the minority lending, he was merely giving lip service to it.

Once again, it was clear that senior leaders were still not on board with recognizing and including minorities; even the Human Resource leaders were in denial about the idea.

I wasn't offered a leadership role with UGI in Charlotte. I was never given a reason, but once again I knew I was being racially blocked. Again, I was asking "How could this be?" "How is it that Leaders and teams of lesser ability continue to move up in organizations, yet the teams of color keep getting denied?"

I knew the answers to my questions, and I continued to remind myself what my mentors had told me, "Recognize the struggle, be prepared and don't give up".

CHAPTER 6:

"MAGIC FOR MINORITIES!"

It was in Oakland, California that I began to work with Magic Johnson's "Pride of Homeownership" program, lending to Minority markets in the Bay Area.

Washington Mutual had emerged as a major lender and had made a tremendous commitment to Minority Lending in major cities like Los Angeles, Atlanta, Chicago, Miami and Oakland.

Recruiters, knowing of my passion for lending to improve the financial well being of people of color, wanted me to build and lead a team in Oakland to drive the Magic Johnson Pride of Homeownership vision.

We built an all-inclusive team. Our team represented the city not the corporation.

We created home ownership for people of color and, just as important, we built stronger more valuable careers for employees of color. This formed the basis for a strong team of Latino, African and Asian Americans.

Success and pride followed.

The results of this team met and exceeded

corporate expectations.

We were finally seeing some hope, some increased opportunities.

I was happy with what we had accomplished over the years, but I also felt some frustration.

I still had not seen any real leadership movement for people of color and I very seldom saw plans to move in that direction. In fact, my boss in Oakland who oversaw the west coast operation was let go. He was an African-American who had been pressing the organization for a greater role. He was now being seen as a threat.

His replacement came from the inner circle, a white leader.

THE WELLS FARGO MORTGAGE ERA, 2006-2018

By now I was recognized as a seasoned, successful leader in the mortgage business.

I had seen my share of success and disappointment. I knew there was still a lot of work to be done. On the job discrimination and inner circle office cliques were rampant. This was true across the board, for people like me and for others who were trying to break through the White Ceiling.

The White Ceiling like the Glass Ceiling was specific. It was made up of white middle and senior leaders who were part of an inner circle that was unbreakable.

Wells Fargo wanted me to lead a team in a minority area. I turned them down because I didn't see that as an opportunity to improve equality. This was again, an example of a major bank thinking they can do their community part by keeping people of color in separate markets from white markets.

They returned with an offer for me to build a mortgage operation team in Northern California. Having just built a strong team in Oakland and knowing the Bay Area market, I liked what they wanted to build and who it could support.

The Bay Area Sales team was strong but with the right partnership it could be the strongest in the mortgage division.

I took the job. We built a team of brown and black people. We built a strong relationship with our sales partners in that region that led them to become the most productive team in the country. The leader of that team went on to lead the Southeastern United States sales organization.

My leadership influence grew. I led teams from San Diego, Sacramento, Oregon, Arizona and Hawaii.

I was doing well; I was ready for the next opportunity.

But I was running into roadblocks; delays and resistance that was evidence of thinly veiled, corporate America racism.

I was warned by a trusted leader that I was going to meet with resistance and get push back. He had been with the organization for several years; he knew the culture and he knew there would be blocks.

Before I was promoted to Senior VP in 2012, I was told by a white female senior leader that I had to take an ESL (English as Second Language) class, so that I could be understood. That was blatant harassment, and it didn't stop there. At another senior conference a white male senior leader called me, out loud, "Buckwheat" a derogatory term towards people of color.

That verbal attack came at me because I was questioning a process that a white female manager was proposing. Prior to that meeting I was told by a white female leader that the company had to "dummy down the job" so that I would get promoted.

All these leaders were in the inner circle. They had all been with the company for some time and now they were facing me. They knew my passion for work and my passion for doing what's right for people of color.

With all this I was more determined than ever to not give up and to see this through. I wasn't going away; I was still going to fight for what I knew was right.

I applied for several leadership roles that I was qualified for; I didn't get a one! They all went to white males. The block was strong. No one could tell me why I wasn't moving forward. Our results were good. Production was high, costs were low. Our ratings were good.

To try and demonstrate my commitment I moved to Orlando, Florida to replace a white leader who had failed to produce. That leader came from the inner circle and received this assignment over me. He failed and now I was taking over. I thought that if I could step out of my comfort zone and lead a successful team then maybe someone in Executive Leadership would recognize that I was the kind of leader, regardless of color, who could build a culture of trust and respect.

I was warned by a trusted associate that the South was

very different and to be careful. He was right!

When I got down South, I was able to overcome the inner circle mentality; I was successful in leading the Florida team to more success.

For the first time in my life, I saw how different one region was from the other in different parts of the country.

On the weekend I would often drive to different cities in Florida so I could get a better understanding of the housing market. What I saw there was almost a re-enactment of the Civil War; houses proudly flying the Confederate Flag!

Now I understood what my associate was talking about.

With my success in Florida the organization asked me to lead the Operation Center in Charlotte North Carolina. That center was a cornerstone for the bank. I remember applying for that role while I was still on the West Coast. I didn't get the job. An inner circle white male got the job and now I was coming in to take his place because he failed, badly.

Again no one could explain to me why I was passed over and now was asked to come in. I didn't dwell on the reasons; I just knew this was going to be another "trial by firing" the white leader that I would replace!

Like all my other assignments in Charlotte I created a better and more inclusive work environment. I did this through communication, trust, follow through, respect and integrity. This was new for them but old hat for me; they never had an organization built on those values before.

(It's important to understand that home loan sales drive the mortgage business.)

Our sales partners grew to respect what we were doing, they believed in us. The feeling was mutual. That leadership role wasn't easy but, like always and unlike others, I told the truth.

Our teams drove high productivity numbers at the least cost. With those results we proved our value and worth to the organization.

Like all my other assignments I worked "with" the teams. Many of these people were people of color; they could see that I was with them in their journey. They knew that when I spoke, I was telling the truth and I was providing my support to help make them better. Making them better would allow them and their families a better more, secure way of life.

I believed that and now I was providing a path for them to accomplish their American Dream of equality and growth.

Yet, it wasn't an immediate win in Charlotte; we had to improve our communication, our follow through and our commitment to the task; it took time, but we did it.

CHAPTER 7:

WINNING AT ALL COSTS!

Two things happened that gave me a different outlook on life. (1) Because of my success in the banking and mortgage industry I knew that I could lead a large organization and (2) I knew that there would be more opportunities to do so.

But before all this I would have to face the reality of my new boss at Wells Fargo. He came from large competitor where he left by mutual agreement. You know what I mean. My guess was there was some disagreement and possibly some harassment involved.

He and I didn't get along. He was in the inner circle, I wasn't. He was white, I wasn't. When he joined the company, I outperformed him in production and cost reduction methods. The major difference between he and I was that I believed in the workers and people of color, both from the operations and sales side. He didn't. He had no respect for the workers. I challenged him on being a racist, he denied it. I was building a culture of partnership in the Southeast; he was blocking my efforts.

One example of this was in a management meeting where he had a verbal confrontation with our only African American sales manager. The confrontation had to do with the concept of service. My boss had no idea what the Sales manager was talking about.

It was clear to me that the Sales manager could see that this leader felt he was better than him so "don't question him". It was also clear that this leader didn't approach or talk to the white operation/sales leaders that way.

I talked to my boss about his behavior; he denied that there was a difference in the way he dealt with his people. I questioned him about his thoughts on affirmative action. His response was that if I had a problem, I should take it up with HR. He had no clue that for a senior leader that response was completely inappropriate; for him that's just the way it was.

THE HEART OF THE MATTER

As time went on, I knew that I could manage whatever task I chose and whatever came my way but there was one thing that I couldn't control: my heart!

I knew that through my experience and ability to understand the value of people that I could make a difference. I also knew that as a Latino and a person of color who had built business relationships and partnerships over the years that I was missing a very important piece of a very necessary foundation.

A critical foundation. It's not something that I intentionally neglected but it became very clear that it was missing.

That foundation was family.

In my career I exuded energy and spirit. I loved working with workers, and I loved challenging the status quo.

Up to now I was providing the energy and spirit that was needed. But what I needed now had to come from my family.

I was told that my heart was weak. Very weak. Within several days I had major heart surgery. I was out of the business for six months. I had no idea that I was that close to my maker.

My family, who I had not intentionally grown apart from, now came alongside me. They provided the support, the love and strength that I had needed all along but figured I could do it alone.

With that in place I knew I could keep making a difference, not necessarily as a leader in my industry. My new, strong heart was now ready for the ongoing fight for equality.

I had forgotten how important the family is in my culture. My family and I were now finally coming together in support of one another.

But it was during this time that I decided to leave the business world.

In leaving I knew the fight wasn't over; people of color still had a long way to go before anything resembling equality was going to happen.

During my exit interview with the Wells Fargo Human Resources rep, she and I debated on what is now called "Diversity and Inclusion."

She said it's real, it exists, and it works; I disagreed and told her I'm living proof that it doesn't!

From then on, I would play a different, less direct but an equally as important role, that of educating, encouraging and mentoring my brothers and sisters of color.

CHAPTER 8:

RETIREMENT: NOW WHAT?

I retired June 6, 2018.

Three years later I had an opportunity to join a major Latino non-profit organization as a consultant.

This non-profit organization works with the Latino community, to ready them for success in a world that so many of us aren't ready for or capable of tackling.

The organization has my passion for helping Latinos and other people of color.

Since I had long seen neglect for people of color, I knew right away that this was the kind of place that I was looking for. This place would give me a chance to help, without fear of the kind of distracting, poisonous corporate-speak of politics or fear of being told that we can't do this or that.

My role was clear. I shared what I saw happening in the world of Finance, Banking and Mortgage. If I was going to help people of color, I had to pass on my knowledge in these areas to the people.

We needed an equal playing field. We needed the rules

to apply to everyone, not just to those who society deems worthy because of their ethnicity or color, or lack of color.

I needed to pass on the rules to those who don't know the rules so they can learn and play by them.

The work is challenging. The employees of the organization are some of the most dedicated individuals I have ever been associated with. The work they do is time consuming and at times, frustrating.

Every day they reach out to the community, providing knowledge and guidance. Helping the community find a path to homeownership.

MY ROLE WITH THE NON-PROFIT

I shared the processes that banks, and lenders use when granting credit to people that leads to homeownership with this team.

But it doesn't start or end there. I also share with them the people and organizations that work with these processes.

- I share the roles that mortgages play in home ownership
- From the Loan Officer to the Funder
- I share with them the various types of loans from Fixed to Adjustable-rate loans
- This includes knowing what a conforming loan is and
- What a nonconforming loan is
- This is fundamental knowledge of home ownership

KNOWLEDGE CREATES OPPORTUNITY

- The knowledge of lending and credit risk
- The roles that Fannie Mae and Freddie Mac play in home ownership
- This information is critical to people of color achieving their American Dream!

We're a long way from what I see as success. But the important thing is that this team is in the game.

It feels good to be part of this team. They've been at it for some time and I'm counting on my experience helping them.

It's organizations like this that can give Latinos and people of color hope. Their work is hard but valuable so in a small way I'm sharing what I can.

CHAPTER 9:

CLEARING THE HURDLES

I've been in this business over 40 years, and I've seen first-hand the prejudice and inequality that Latinos and people of color face.

In my role as a support person, I have been able to lay out for them the various processes that Banks and Lenders participate in when evaluating customers for income and credit risk.

These steps allow the consumer the opportunity to purchase a home and build wealth.

This process has not always been available for the Latino community and people of color.

Since joining this organization I've had conversations with the team members about the kind of barriers that Latinos face in pursuing wealth equality.

Those barriers are often so well-disguised that the clients don't even know they're being blocked from the kind of knowledge that will allow them to succeed!

CHAPTER 10:

THE DREAMERS

Working with the non-profit has given me a better picture of what it means to try and achieve the American Dream.

One of my teammates is a "Dreamer". This young man is a Latino that was brought to this country at a young age by their immigrant parents. He's not a citizen yet he went to school in the US from first grade all the way to college. He tells me he feels like an American he acts like an American yet he's not a citizen.

Many Dreamers have no ties to their birth land, and many have never returned. Some have served in the military, and some have died for this country. They can't vote. They work in many different fields at various levels.

Active Dreamers range in age 20-40.

President Obama felt like he could help the Dreamers but because of resistance that he encountered it was difficult. President Trump wanted to send them back to their countries. President Biden is working to help them become citizens.

The general feeling among Dreamers is that they want to stay in the US and become citizens.

I see this situation like when the first Europeans came to America; they found themselves without a country but with an opportunity to be part of this country. That was the start of a long process for most of them.

I see no difference between then and now, especially since many of the Dreamers parents are the laborers in this country, doing the work to keep this country alive and prospering.

In my role I've been able to outline for the team the various processes that Banks and Lenders participate in when evaluating income and credit risks.

These steps allow the consumer the opportunity to purchase a home and develop wealth.

For the Latino community and communities of color that process has not always been successful.

These employees have seen the blocks that are presented to the Latino community.

Yet they continue to commit themselves to make a difference and drive towards equality.

IT'S ABOUT MORE THAN THE DREAMERS

Latinas born and raised in America are also striving for equality.

These two people mentioned below shared their experience with me; they're examples of how Latinas see the fight they have ahead of them.

One is in a leadership role and the other isn't.

Before joining the nonprofit, this young Latina who's not in a leadership role, saw major differences from her prior role. She saw differences in communication and attitude towards people of color versus white clients. She would ask why, and she would get the same response I got in Corporate America.

She saw people of color being charged more for services versus white clients and she saw more commitments made by her company to white customers than to Latino customers. When she joined this team, it gave her an opportunity to change that pattern.

Her Latino partner is in the health industry, and he sees very few people of color in leadership roles, decision-making roles. Again no one provides a reason why.

CHAPTER 11:

RAMPANT RACISM?

Over the last several months I have had many conversations with one of the current leaders in the non-profit organization.

It's apparent that this Latina is fully committed to the cause of bettering the lives of people of color.

As I was relating to her a recent experience I had regarding racism, she told me a story.

Her parents migrated from Mexico and never asked for help. They worked hard, saved their money and made sure that their children grew up to be responsible, successful citizens. And that's exactly what she's been doing.

When she was growing up in very humble beginnings, she had a best friend who she was close to.

This friend's family had a good life and they welcomed her into their family circle.

They remained friends for many years.

She respected her friend and the family. She felt loved and safe.

Then came the election of 2016.

It was during the pre-election period that another side of her friend and the family began to show itself.

The family decided it was time to let her know where they really stood. Their true feelings came out full force!

She felt betrayed, hurt and angry. The family's racism had been hidden all these years and now, she found out what they really felt about people of color.

I assured her that she belonged and that she has every right as her friend. I also told her that I wasn't surprised that her friend and her family had that attitude about race.

I too knew that racism has been hiding and when it came down to it if those people are racist, it will come out like it did for her; I've seen this too many times to count.

CHAPTER 12:

WHAT'S NEXT?

Recently I decided to visit San Diego, a city that has a good mix of people. This would also give me a chance to travel, and breath some air, cooler than Arizona's.

After I arrived in San Diego, I was hungry so I went to a restaurant.

I sat down next to a couple about my age from out of state.

We started talking about America and what's happening to our country. They told me about their background and where they grew up. That led to talking about me and my background as well.

As the conversation went on, I sensed that they didn't understand when I talked about race relations in America. We talked about the recent Black Lives Matter activity and about the January 6th insurrection.

The talk was serious yet open. After listening to their opinions on the issues, I felt some frustration as I offered my opinions.

We talked about relationships with the police. They

questioned me how I felt about the police, and I told them that I believe that the police are needed to protect and serve.

I also shared with them that in communities of color there may be a different understanding of policing. I don't think they liked my answer.

We continued to talk about the differences between white communities and non-white communities. I listened and they listened.

It was a good exchange of information and understanding. We talked about today's America and who the real Americans are.

They struggled with their answers. I was getting the impression that their idea of America may not include people of color. I didn't press the issue, I just continued to listen.

Then we got into a discussion about our borders. The more we talked about this subject the more it was obvious to me that they favored closed borders.

They didn't say why. But the more we talked the more I was convinced that they wanted 100% closed borders.

I responded by saying the United States grew from immigrants and I see the border struggle as just another form of seeking opportunity.

I went a little deeper with them in trying to compare what's going on at the borders today to when it was possible that many of their distant relatives came to America from Europe or elsewhere.

They didn't want to accept that comparison. I wanted to know why but they didn't have an answer.

They believed and voiced exactly what Donald Trump

said that "these people are drug smugglers and rapists".

I explained to them that when you look at the face of America today you see an increase of people of color. And those people are either Americans or someday they will be.

I also told them that some may never become citizens but that's where decisions about them must be made in a respectful manner. All people must be treated with dignity. They agreed that all people no matter what color should be treated with dignity and respect.

I acknowledged that comment and I thanked them for their understanding. I also reminded them that many people of color coming to the States turn out to be gardeners, house cleaners and other helpers in the communities. Overall, they'll take jobs that no one wants.

They had no response to what I was telling them. What I was saying is that people of color, whether they're citizens or not, are all trying to achieve a better way of life just like they and their families are trying to do.

As it turned out their idea of America is driven by their own color, or lack of it. Based on our conversation it seemed to me that they feel like the United States is meant to be a place for people like them and them only.

As we finished our conversation, I asked them to try and understand that this is America and people of color have played a major role in the development and success of the country.

As I was leaving, I thanked them for the spirited conversation and for the knowledge I gained. I also told them I hoped they had a better understanding, from my perspective, of what this country is all about.

Then I paid for their food and drinks, hoping my gesture of goodwill would continue to open their minds to what I had told them.

That caught them by surprise!

I could tell by the looks on their faces that they felt like "How could this person of color who they just met be willing to pay for their meal after such a conversation?"

For me it was just the right thing to do.

AFTERWORD

The journey continues. I have no choice. There are things I can't forget.

I can't forget what I saw riding the bus every morning in 1966.

I can't forget seeing the faces of the hundreds of Latinos and people of color riding public transportation to jobs that will help them support their families and their dreams.

I can't forget crossing the 3rd street bridge and seeing the massive change in the financial landscape.

I can't forget the real reasons why we were allowed to join the financial softball league; to be used by a company because it gave them inner circle bragging rights!

I can't forget what little part, if any, Latinos played in the Affirmative Action and Equal Opportunity programs.

I saw the same type of exclusion just 4 years ago, when the big banks and corporations talked about "Diversity and Inclusion;" paying lip service to that "idea".

The real challenge for Latinos and other persons of color on their path to real leadership will be to help pave the way for others.

It was only a couple of years ago that Wells Fargo's newly hired CEO was interviewed and asked about "Diversity and Inclusion."

He stated that "You can't find qualified African-American candidates to hire into the more Senior Leadership roles".

That way of thinking has gone on for years. Their results have been lousy, yet the corporations will defend their human resource records. The sad part is that if you offer a solution, it usually falls on deaf ears.

I know this because it was only a few years ago that I reached out to the new CEO and other Senior Leaders offering my help to change the culture and make inclusion a reality. I never got a response; not even a "thank you, or no thank you."

I still hear the voices of people of color asking, "How can I succeed, how can I get ahead? What do I have to do?"

Why is it that the inner circle succeeds, and we as brown and black people don't?

How can we not be equal in wealth, health and education? Why are there still blocks to us in 2022?

Our job is to be aware of those blocks and prepare ourselves to challenge them.

We can't give up. The teams I supported on my journey heard me say time and again, "Don't give up!" Because that's exactly what the "inner circle" leaders want you to do.

The American Dream is real. You have a right to it. A right for equal wealth, education, health and community. I didn't get a college degree but if you can get one, do it.

Don't let that block you.

If you don't pursue your education, train yourself, seek guidance and be the best you can be in that pursuit.

I hope that reading about my journey opens your eyes to what's ahead as you carve your path towards equality.

Share your passion for excellence, make a difference because that passion not only helps you, but it deeply affects and influences other Latinos and people of color.

This is your country; you have rights and opportunities to pursue your dreams, use these as tools to create your future.

But be aware of what surrounds you, prepare yourself for the resistance with knowledge and drive.

GO BIG OR STAY HOME!

It was just the summer of 2021 that my wife and I were confronted with racism as we were shopping at a well-known big-box store.

We had just finished shopping and were in the check-out line to pay. As we moved closer to the register, practicing social distancing and wearing our masks, I noticed a white woman without a mask moving quickly toward our line.

She looked angry. As she moved closer to our line, she barged in front of a person of color who had been behind us, practicing social distancing.

When she did this, I reminded her that there was a

line.

She looked at my wife and with hate in her eyes, she said that we didn't belong in this country; that we were peasants and that we needed to go back where we came from.

You have what you need to succeed; I ask you to remember my story and know that you too can accomplish whatever you need with respect and trust.

But most important, always keep in mind the need to "pay it forward" whatever success you attain, as you make the necessary steps to success.

Never give up!
Alex Vasquez

www.ingramcontent.com/pod-product-compliance
Lightning Source LLC
Chambersburg PA
CBHW070318220526
45465CB00004B/1897